*litiae species amor est.*

OVID

*ne capiet;*

*flava*

PLAUTUS C.250–184 B

*ic ubi amore noees?*

*Nec meum respectum, ut ante,*
*amorem,*
*Qui illius culpa cecedit.*

70–19 BC

CATULLUS C.84–54 BC

# ARS AMORIS

*Latin for Lovers*

# ARS AMORIS

*Latin for Lovers*

Sean McMahon
Illustrated by Anne M. Anderson

Appletree Press

First published in 1998 by
The Appletree Press Ltd,
19-21 Alfred Street,
Belfast, BT2 8DL
Tel: +44 (0) 1232 243074
Fax: +44 (0) 1232 256756
Web Site: www.irelandseye.com
E-mail: frontdesk@appletree.ie

**Ars Amoris – Latin for Lovers**

A catalogue record for this book is available from the British Library.

ISBN 0-86281-665-3

9 8 7 6 5 4 3 2 1

# Contents

# Virginibus Puerisque

**For young people**

*Amor tussisque non celantur.*

Love and a cough cannot be hidden.

ANON

*Dulce est desipere*
*Et carpamus dulcia*
*Iuventutis tenere.*

It is great to act the fool; so let us hold on to all the sweet pleasures of youth.

CARMINA BURANA, ANON, 13TH CENTURY

# Formosam resonare doces Amaryllida silvas.

You teach the woods to echo the name of Amaryllis.

VIRGIL 70–19 BC

*Tempus est iocundum*
*O virgines,*
*Modo congaudete*
*Vos iuvenes*

*O O totus floreo*
*Iam amore virginali*
*Totus ardeo*
*Novus, novus*
*amor*
*Est quo pereo*

Now is the time for fun, girls. You young ones enjoy yourselves! Oh, Oh! I am blooming with the love of girls. Oh brother! I am aflame with new love and it's killing me.

CARMINA BURANA, ANON, 13TH CENTURY

*Verba dat omnis amor reperitque*
*alimenta morando.*

All love supplies the words and finds
sustenance in delay.

OVID 43 BC–AD C.17

*Tandem destine matrem*
*Tempestiva sequi viro.*

Time to leave your mother, dear;
you're ready for a man!

HORACE 65-8 BC

# Procul hinc, procul este, severae!

Keep away, far away, you sour-faced women.

OVID 43 BC–AD C.17

# Homo totiens moritur quotiens amittit suos.

You die a little when you lose someone you love.

PUBILIUS SYRUS FL. IST CENTURY BC

# Virginibus puerisque canto.

I sing for youth!

HORACE 65–8 BC

*Candida me capiet;*
*capiet me flava puella.*

I'm a sucker for a blonde – and
for a brunette!

OVID 43 BC–AD C.17

# Cum ames non sapias aut cum sapias non ames.

When you love you can't think and when you can think you can't be in love.

PUBILIUS SYRUS *FL.* 1ST CENTURY BC

# Amor ut lacrima ab oculo oritur in pectus cadit.

Love, like a tear, starts in the eye and falls on the bosom.

PUBILIUS SYRUS *FL.* 1ST CENTURY BC

*Ab amante lacrimis
redimas iracundiam.*

Tears can soften a lover's rage.

PUBILIUS SYRUS *FL* 1ST CENTURY BC

*O formose puer,*
*nimium ne crede*
*colori.*

Don't bank too much
on your complexion,
lovely boy.

VIRGIL  70–19 BC

*Malo me Galatea*
*petit, lasciva puella,*
*Et fugit ad salices et*
*se cupit ante videri.*

Galatea, the saucy piece, throws apples
at me and then runs and hides in the
willows. But she makes sure I've seen
her!

VIRGIL 70–19 BC

# Amare et sapere vix conceditur.

To love and be wise isn't given even to the gods.

PUBILIUS SYRUS *FL.* 1ST CENTURY BC

# Succesore novo vincitur omnis amor.

Old love is always vanquished by a new one.

OVID 43 BC–AD C.17

# Credula res amor est.

In love you'll believe anything.

OVID 43 BC–AD C.17

# Tolle cupidinem
# Immitis uvae.

Keep away from unripe grapes!

HORACE 65-8 BC

*Fabas indulcet fames.*

Hunger makes even beans tasty.

ANON

# Quarebam
## quid Amarem

I looked for someone to love

*Pulchra comis annisque decens*

*et candida vultu*

*Dulce quiescenti basia*

*blanda dabas.*

*Si te iam vigilans non unquam*

*cernere possum*

*Somne, precor, iugitur nostra tene.*

Young, blonde and beautiful, you gave me sweet kisses as I slept. If when I wake I'll never actually see you, then god of sleep, I ask that you keep me dreaming for ever.

ANON 9TH CENTURY AD

23

*Huc vina et unguenta et nimium breves*

*Flores amoenae ferre iube rosae,*

*Dum res et aetas et sororum*

*Fila trium patiuntur atra.*

Bring wine and oil and roses, those flowers that
fade too soon, while we have cash and strength and
before those cruel Fates cut the thread.

HORACE 65–8 BC

*Nondum amabam,*
*et amare*
*amabam...quaerebam*
*quid amarem,*
*amans amare.*

I had not fallen in love but I loved to be
in love; I looked for someone to love,
loving to love.

ST AUGUSTINE AD C.354–430

**Lydia, dic, per omnes**
**Te deos oro, Sybarin cur properes amando**
**perdere?**

For God's sake tell me, Lydia, why are you
killing Sybaris with love?

HORACE 65–8 BC

*Iuppiter ex alto*
*peruriae ridet*
*amantium*

**Jove on high laughs at the antics of
lovers.**

OVID  43 BC–AD C.17

*Commodat in lusus*
*numina surda Venus.*

**Venus winks at lovers' games.**

OVID 43 BC–AD C.17

*Quid iste tuus praeter nova carmina vates? Amatoris milia multa leges.*

What does your poet give you apart from new songs? Lots of handy chat-up lines for you to read.

OVID 43 BC–AD C.17

*Pereant...qui ante nos nostra dixerunt.*

Damn those who got in first with *our* remarks.

AELIUS DONATUS 4TH CENTURY AD

*Ignoranti, quem portum petat, nullus suus ventus est.*

For those who don't know which port
they're heading to no wind is favourable.

SENECA THE YOUNGER c. 4 BC–AD 65

**Blanditia non imperio fit dulcis Venus.**

Love is made sweet by charm not bossiness.

PUBILIUS SYRUS FL. 1ST CENTURY BC

*Littore quot conchae tot sunt in amore dolores.*

There are as many sorrows in love as there are shells on the seashore.

OVID 43 BC–AD C.17

# Nec te quaesiveris extra.

Take no heed of any opinions but your own.

PERSIUS AD 34–62


# Non tibi ab ancilla est incipienda venus.

When wooing, don't start with the maid.

OVID 43 BC–AD C.17

# *Animo virum pudicae non oculo eligunt*

Judicious women choose a man using
the head rather than the eye.

PUBILIUS SYRUS *FL.* 1ST CENTURY BC

# *Arte perennat amor.*

Love is preserved by skills.

PUBILIUS SYRUS *FL.* 1ST CENTURY BC

*Insequeris, fugio; fugis insequor; haec mihi mens est.*

If you come on, I'll run away; if you run away, I'll follow. That's the way my mind works.

MARTIAL AD c.40–c.104

# Nox et Amor

Night and love

Nox et Amor

*O blandos oculos et inquietos*
*Et quadam propria nota loquaces.*

O lovely dancing eyes that speak without a
tongue.

ANON, 9TH CENTURY

*Cras amet qui nunquam amavit,*
*quique amavit cras amet.*

Tomorrow let both him who has
never loved and him who has often
loved, love again.

FROM *PERVIGILIUM VENERIS*, 3RD CENTURY

# *Amore nihil mollius nihil violentius.*

Nothing is tamer nor wilder than love.

ANON

*Iam, dulcis amica, venito*

*Quam sicut cor meum diligo;*

*Intra in cubiculum meum*

*Ornamentis cunctis onustum.*

*Ibi sunt sedilia strata*

*Et domus velis ornata*

*Floresque in domo sparguntur*

*Herbes fragrantes miscentur.*

Come darling now, you love of my heart. Come into my bedroom, all adorned for your delight. The couches are laid out, the place decently veiled, scattered with flowers mixed with sweet herbs.

ANON, 10TH CENTURY

*Sedit in ore*
*Rosa cum pudore,*
*Pulsatus amore*
*Quod os lamberem.*

Beauty sits on her mouth red with her shame. I,
shaking with love, want to quench my thirst on
that mouth.

CARMINA BURANA, ANON, 13TH CENTURY

*Da mihi castitatem et continentiam, sed noli modo.*

Give me chastity and continency – but not just yet!

ST AUGUSTINE AD c.354–430

**Dulce ridentem Lalagen amabo**
**Dulce loquentem.**

Ever will I love Lalage with her sweet laughter and talk.

HORACE 65–8 BC

*Vivemus, mea Lesbia,*

*atque amemus,*

*Rumoresque senum severiorum*

*Omnes unius aestimemus assis.*

*Solis occidere et redire possunt*

*Nobis cum semel occidit brevis lux*

*Nox est perpetua una dormienda.*

Let us live and love, my Lesbia, and consider the
opinions of sour old people as worth no more
than a cent. Suns will rise and suns will set but
when our short light is spent, we'll have to sleep
in endless night.

CATULLUS C.84–C.54 BC

*Omnia vincit Amor: et nos cedamus Amori.*

Love is master of everything;
let us too yield to love.

VIRGIL 70–19 BC

*Nunc iuvat in teneris dominae iacuisse lacertis.*

Now it is sweet to lie in the tender
arms of your love.

OVID 43 BC–AD C.17

*Urit me Glycerae nitor*
*Splenditis Pario*
*marmore purius:*
*Urit grata protervitas*
*Et vultus nimium*
*lubricus aspici.*

The glitter of Glycera blinds me, brighter
than Parian stone – those teasing tricks,
that sexy dazzling face!

HORACE 65–8 BC

*Da mihi mille basia,*
*deinde centum,*
*Dein mille altera, dein*
*secunda centum*
*Deinde usque altera,*
*deinde centum.*

Give me a thousand kisses,
then a hundred;
another thousand, a second hundred;
yet another thousand
and still a hundred more.

HORACE 65–8 BC

# Nox at amor vinumque nihil moderabile suadent.

Night and love and wine don't teach restraint.

OVID 43 BC–AD c.17

*Blanditia molles,*
*auremque iuvantia*
*verba adfer.*
*Si poteris vere, si minus*
*apta tamen.*

With soft persuasions and coaxing words,
assault the ear.
Tell the truth if possible; if not,
do the best you can.

OVID 43 BC–AD C.17

*Dilige et quod vis fac.*

**Love and do what you want.**

ST AUGUSTINE AD c.354–430


*Qualis nox fuit illa,*
*di deaeque,*
*Quam mollis torus.*
*Haesimus calentes.*

**Ye gods what a night that was! How springy the bed, how hotly we clung.**

PETRONIUS ARBITER D. AD 65

*Qui amat, si esurit,*
*nullam esurit.*

The lover when hungry isn't really
hungry.

PLAUTUS c.250–184 BC


*...sic sic sine fine feriati*
*Et tecum iaceamus*
*osculantes.*

Thus on holiday, let's lie and kiss our fill.

PETRONIUS ARBITER D. AD 65

# Capistrum Maritale
### The matrimonial halter

*Silentium mulieri praestat ornatum.*

**Silence is a woman's best adornment.**

ANON

*Adhibenda in iocanda moderatio.*

Don't carry a joke too far.

Cicero 106–43 bc

*Uxor vivamus ut viximus et teneamus*

*Nomina quae primo sumpsimus*

*in thalamo;*

*Nec ferat ulla dies, ut commutemur*

*in aevo,*

*Quin tibi sim iuvenis tuque*

*puella mihi.*

Wife, let us live as we've always done and still use the pet names we used on our honeymoon. I hope that day will never come when I'll not be your suitor and you my lady.

Ausonius ad c.310–c.393

# Quod quis habet, dominae conferat omne suae.

Whatever a fellow has let him give it
to the love of his life.

OVID 43 BC–AD C.17

*Ergo age duremus, quamvis adolverit aetas,*
*Utamurque annis quos mora parva teret.*
*Fas et iura veteres extendere amores.*

So still let us love though the years are passing
and use the years that brief delay is wasting. It is
right and proper that old love should last.

PETRONIUS ARBITER D. AD 65

## Concordia Discors.

Harmony in discord.

HORACE 65–8 BC

### *Militiae species amor est.*

Love is a kind of warfare.

OVID 43 BC–AD C.17

# Amantium irae amoris integratio est.

Lovers' quarrels are love's best cement.

TERENCE C.190–159 BC

## Parentes plus amant filios quam e converso.

Parents love their children more than children love them.

ANON

# Non caret effectu, quod volere duo.

Nothing can stop what two people decide to do.

OVID 43 BC–AD C.17

# *Nunc scio quid sit Amor.*

**Now I know what love is!**

VIRGIL 70–19 BC

# Capistrum maritale.

**The matrimonial halter.**

JUVENAL *FL.* 2ND CENTURY AD

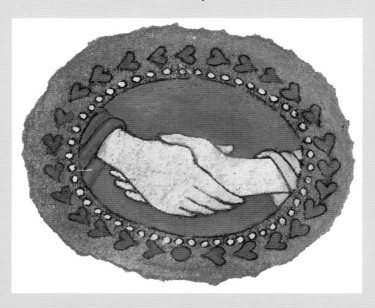

*Consueduto*
*concinnat amorem.*

Familiarity breeds!
(Literally habit causes love.)

PUBILIUS *FL*. 1ST CENTURY BC


*Fas et iura sinunt veteres*
*extendere amores.*

Both justice and the laws insist that old loves
should last.

PETRONIUS ARBITER D. AD 65

# Odi et Amo

**I hate and I love**

*In omni adversitate fortunae*
*infelicissium est genus infortunii,*
*fuisse felicem.*

In any misfortune the most unhappy
kind of unfortunate man is the one who
used to be happy.

BOETHIUS AD C.476–524

*Sed mulier cupido quod*
*dicit amanti,*
*In vento et rapida*
*scribere oportet aqua.*

A woman's lovetalk to her sweetheart should be
written in wind and rushing water.

CATULLUS C.84–54 BC

# Vindicta
## Nemo magis gaudet quam femina.

Nobody enjoys getting even more than a woman.

JUVENAL *FL.* 2ND CENTURY AD

*Quid facies odio sic ubi amore noces?*

**What will you be like hating when you are so nasty loving?**

OVID 43 BC–AD C.17

*Odi et amo: quare id faciam, fortasse requiris. Nescio, sed fieri sentio et excrucior.*

I hate and I love. You'll want to know why.
I don't know – but that's how I feel and it's hell!

CATULLUS C.84–54 BC

*Nec meum respectum, ut ante, amorem,*
*Qui illius culpa cecedit.*

Don't look back to find my love,
that wilted through her fault.

CATULLUS C.84–54 BC

*Et taedat Veneris*
*statim peractae.*

The pleasure of sex is brief and gross,
and weariness follows after.

PETRONIUS ARBITER D. AD 65


*Qui finem quaeris amoris,*
*Cedat amor rebus;*
*res age, tutus eris.*

You there who wants to be free of love,
know this: love will yield to business; keep busy
and you'll be all right.

OVID 43 BC–AD C.17

*Possessa ferus pectora versat amor.*

Cruel love tortures the heart it rules.

OVID 43 BC–AD C.17

VARIVM ET MVTABILE
SEMPER FEMINA

*At regina [Dido] gravi
iamdudum saucia cura
volnus alit venis et caeco
carpitur igni.*

But the queen [Dido] had for a long
time now been torn by love's deadly
hurt, feeding it with her blood and
eaten up by its unseen fire.

VIRGIL 70–19 BC

# *Varium et mutabile semper Femina.*

Woman is fickle.

VIRGIL 70–19 BC

*Amans, amens!*

Lover, lunatic!

PLAUTUS C.250–184 BC

*...cum frigida mors*
*anima seduxerit artus*
*Omnibus umbra*
*locis adero, dabis,*
*improbe, poenas;*
*Audiam, et haec*
*manes veniet mihi*
*fama sub imos.*

When death's icy hand shall take the life from
my body, my ghost shall be with you everywhere.
You will be punished for your misdeeds
and I shall hear, for the news will reach me
among the dead.

VIRGIL 70–19 BC

*Aliudque cupido
mens aliud
suadet.*

The heart and the head send
different signals.

PLAUTUS c.250–184 BC

*O crudelis Alexi, nihil
mea carmina curas?
Nil nostri miserere?
Mori me denique coges.*

Cruel Alexis, you don't like my love verses.
You have no pity for me and you'll kill me
in the end.

VIRGIL 70–19 BC

*Sed Haec*
*Prius Fuere*

# Sed Haec
# Prius Fuere

**But that's all over now**

*Post coitum omne animal est triste.*

After love-making every animal is sad.

ANON

# Tempora mutantur,
# et nos mutamur in illis.

Times change – and we change with them.

ANON

*Sero te amavi, pulchritudo*
*tam antiqua et tam nova.*

Late have I loved you,
beauty so old and so new.

ST AUGUSTINE AD C.354–430

TEMPORE MVTANTVR ET

NOS MVTAMVR IN ILLIS

# Amori finem tempus non animus facit.

Time, not the heart, finishes love.

PUBILIUS SYRUS *FL.* 1ST CENTURY BC

*Multi quidem*
*facilius se abstinent*
*ut non utantur,*
*quam temperent ut*
*bene utantur.*

Many find it easier to abstain
completely than to practise decent
moderation.

St Augustine ad c.354–430

*Lusitis satis, edisti satis*
*atque bibisti.*
*Tempus abire ibi est.*

You have played yourself enough, have eaten and
drunk enough. It's time for you to give up!

Horace 65–8 bc

*Vixi puellis nuper*
*idoneusEt militavi non*
*sine gloria:*
*Nunc arma*
*defunctum bello*
*Barbiton hic*
*paries habebit.*

I've been around, until very lately fit for the girls,
and fought the old fight with some glory. Now
my weapons and my armour, like my lute, its
campaigns over, hang there on the wall.

PUBILIUS SYRUS <small>FL.</small> 1ST CENTURY BC

*Sed haec prius fuere.*

**But that's all over now.**
CATULLUS c.84–54 BC

*Quod not cogit amor?*

**Is there anything love couldn't make us do?**
MARTIAL AD c.40–104

*Parcius iunctas quatiunt fenestras*

*Iactibus crebris iuvenes protervi*

*Nec tibi somnos adimunt, amatque*

*Ianua limen*

*Quae prius multum facilis movebat*

*cardines; audis minus et minus iam:*

*'Me tuo longas pereunte noctes*

*Lydia, dormis?'*

The likely lads don't batter your closed shutters
as often nor ruin a good night's sleep. The doors
stick close together that used to swing open so
easily. Less and less frequently do you hear,
'How can you sleep so sound, Lydia, while I
stand all night here?'

PUBILIUS SYRUS FL. 1ST CENTURY BC

*Deleo omnes dehinc
ex animo mulieres.*

From now on I'm going to put women out
of my head.

TERENCE c.190–159 BC

*Meminerunt omnia
amantes.*

Lovers remember everything.

OVID 43 BC–AD c.17

Aliudque cup

aliud suadet. Anon

Candida

capiet me

Quid facies odio

Nunc scio quid sit Am

Amor tussisque